T0381433

The Sunshine Girl

A Mother's Love Story to Her Daughter

DEBRA HARDER

WITH ARTWORK AND POETRY BY JANET SUE COLE

WestBow Press books may be ordered through booksellers or by contacting:

WestBow Press
A Division of Thomas Nelson & Zondervan
1663 Liberty Drive
Bloomington, IN 47403
www.westbowpress.com
1 (866) 928-1240

ISBN: 978-1-9736-3712-7 (sc)
ISBN: 978-1-9736-4354-8 (hc)
ISBN: 978-1-9736-3713-4 (e)

Library of Congress Control Number: 2018909768

Print information available on the last page.

WestBow Press rev. date: 11/26/2018

WestBow
PRESS®
A DIVISION OF THOMAS NELSON
& ZONDERVAN

Poems and paintings by
Janet Sue Cole

June 10, 1981
to
October 3, 2011

A Life Lived and Experienced
A Life Taken All Too Soon

CONTENTS

Foreword ix

Introduction xi

Meadows 1

Moment in Time 9

J. Alfred Prufrock 11

A Tendency toward Reclusiveness 14

Life, Death, and Learning 22

Hopes and Dreams 28

Love, Familial and Romantic 33

Faith 38

Acceptance 44

Reflection and Healing 46

Cancer 51

Conclusion 57

Acknowledgments 59

DEDICATIONS

This book is dedicated to the memory of my daughter, Janet Sue Cole. She lived her life with full determination and spirit. While the impact of Hodgkin's lymphoma treatment may have taken her life, it did not take her spirit. It is also dedicated to the memory of my loving and equally creative mother, Sally Ann Lee, who passed away of pancreatic cancer one month before Janet was diagnosed with Hodgkin's. I also dedicate it to all cancer survivors and to the memory of those who have lost their battles with the wicked disease. Last but far from least, this book is dedicated to the caretakers, families, and friends of those with cancer. While cancer may threaten our physical lives, and of those we love, it cannot take our spirits, hopes, our will to fulfill what we were destined to do, or the footprints we leave behind. May Janet's spirit, and that of all those who have gone before, remain with each of us.

"For I know the plans I have for you," declares the Lord … "plans to prosper you and
not to harm you, plans to give you hope and a future." (Jeremiah 29:11 NIV)

You are my sunshine.
I love you.
Mom

Foreword

The Sunshine Girl is a heartwarming tribute from a mother to her daughter, who lost her life far too soon. As I read through the pages, it was as if Janet were sitting beside me, saying, "Oh, you are going to love this!"

I met Janet the last year of her life. I had been praying that God would plan my days and use me where I could be of service. The following week, in walks Janet. And from that moment on, my life was never the same. I had the privilege of transporting her to chemotherapy treatments at the hospital. It was there that I observed her caring attitude toward other patients, her courage in facing the enemy of cancer, and her determination to live each day to the fullest.

> Though I never chose this path
> I refuse to turn from it in fear.
> — Janet Sue Cole

Sometimes I visited her in the hospital late at night, far past visiting hours. This seemed to be a good time for us as we laughed and talked into the night. When the nurses came into the room, Janet and I shares a look that said, "I dare them to tell me I have to leave." In their wisdom, none of them ever said a word.

Janet was blessed with writing and artistic abilities far beyond her years. She looked at life, with its struggles and craziness, and was able to paint a picture with her words. As you read Janet's poetry, may you come away knowing life is beautiful even when it rains.

Thank you, Janet, for taking the hinges off the shutters in my life. I am a better person for having known you.

Elaine Hull

INTRODUCTION

Janet was born on June 10, 1981, at 7:00 p.m. at Saint Luke's Hospital in Boise, Idaho. She weighed seven pounds five ounces and was twenty inches long. She was a gift from God above. She was dedicated to him on November 1, 1981. Her father and I were so incredibly grateful for our young daughter and sister to her brother, Jim.

She was walking by eleven months of age. As she continued to move and grow, she increasingly demonstrated her rambunctious and strong spirit. She also increasingly demonstrated her sensitive soul, which always sought to help others who were disabled and the children and elderly. She was always grateful for the opportunity to travel to Mexico to help build houses for the poor and loved spending time helping with the young children there. As a teenager and young adult, Janet worked with kids who had special needs and provided home care for the elderly. She was always loyal to her grandparents and made every effort to be available to help them with any needs they had.

In young adulthood, Janet sought her independence with a fiery drive. She struggled with asthma for years, and her independence was always something she struggled to maintain through multiple medical complications and health problems. She was so proud of her apartment and her independence. She was devastated when her Hodgkin's diagnosis forced her to leave her apartment and move to California to live with her mom and stepdad while she obtained treatment for her illness. Most important, she grieved leaving her beloved hometown of Boise, Idaho.

Meadows

As a child, Janet loved to dream, dance in a pretty dress, and play house with a tent she and her brother, Jim, built in the living room.

It is springtime once more.
I remember when as children we would use
dandelions for tea and mud for pies.
Every spring we would roll around the lawn, playing
gypsies and unicorns, and Pegasus
till sundown.
Life was so simple and full of joy.
It's nice to remember.

Dancing with the Faeries J. COLE 10-22-01

Growing up, Janet was always boldly truthful and never afraid to speak her mind. Once when asked to call her grandparents and apologize for being very naughty while staying with them, she did indeed apologize. However, she added her own defiant but truthful moment, saying, "My mom made me say that." Her grandma said that was the sincerest apology she ever got.

So it is that the truth
is in the moment.

And while the truth may change
from one moment to the next,
it is still the truth
in the moment.

And the only truth I will ever know.

Janet had so many God-given talents and was so creative. She loved to draw, paint, read, write poetry, and sing. She planned her life through her drawings, developing ideas with pictures of her hopes for her future. She learned to play the violin in school. Her teacher had to remind her to learn her notes as she had an ear for music and could easily play along with the sound of the music. She could sing like Patsy Cline in "Crazy" and Janis Joplin in "Me and Bobby McGee."

Purple leaves and orange
 flowers drift lazily and
catch in my hair as I
wander unubsthucted through
my meadow.
Did you know I have a
meadow? I do.
You should have a
            meadow too.

As she grew, so did the meadows that were growing within her spirit. They were increasingly demonstrated in her art.

Meadow

Purple leaves and
orange blossoms
drift around and
catch
in my hair
as I wander
unobstructed
thru my meadow.

Did you know I have a meadow?
I do.
You should have a meadow too.

On November 30, 2001 at the age of 20, Janet painted "The Edge of my Meadow," demonstrating her specific idea of "what heaven would be" with "birch trees in meadow grass" and "a trail back home." She wrote that her meadow was as big as her imagination and only when she wants to, does she see the end.

A group of yellow butterflies
leap up towards the sky
    as I pass by.
How pretty.

        Below my feet grow
bunches of red tulips.
        How lovely.

Janet's appreciation for color and detail was evidenced in many areas of her life and our life together. She was always adamant with me about the specific names of colors. If I said something was brown she would correct me and say, "no mom that is burnt sienna." In her painting "Indian Summer" of December 18, 2002 she was most descriptive about her choice of paint colors and the detail of the world around her. Everything had a purpose. The girl is sitting amongst a meadow full of Janet's favorite flowers the black-eyed Susan. The girl has burnt sienna hair and matching freckles on pale pink skin. She is wearing a yellow sundress and is sitting on the blue green grass under the pale orange sky. Flying nearby are the intense blue butterflies and a dragon fly. Janet's addition of the book laying open beside the girl reflects her own love for books. The girl's eyes appear closed as if she is just breathing and taking it all in to the very depths of her soul.

Moment in Time

Janet could take a momentary occurrence and turn it into a lasting visual and sensual memory. You felt you were reexperiencing that one moment just by closing your eyes and listening, or by reading a few of her words on a page. You had an opportunity to breathe and take it all in all over again.

The evening is so peaceful.
It has been raining off and on for days now,
and everything smells fresh and are verdant and moist.
Today, while driving with Mom, it would
rain
and
stop,
rain
and
stop,
every few seconds
as we passed
(under)
each
individual
rain cloud.
It finally let up, so I am sitting with the window open,
just letting it all seep into me.

The lilacs are in bloom
(I do so love the smell of lilacs).
It is a happy thing, spring.

Two robins sat next to

each other

for the longest time

on the lawn today.

They must have had a nice visit.

I wonder what was said.

I guess we'll never know.

J. Alfred Prufrock

While visiting Janet's uncle David for Thanksgiving in 1996, she found a stray male kitten in Lovelock, Nevada. He seemed bound and determined to cling to Janet to avoid the coyotes that frequented the area. After talking me into letting her keep him, we took him back to Meridian. As she was always fond of poetry, she gave him the name J. Alfred Prufrock from the T. S. Eliot poem "The Love Song of J. Alfred Prufrock." J, as he came to be known, was soon able to worm his way into the lives and hearts of every person and animal he came in contact with. Janet loved that cat with her whole heart, and J loved her.

This poem, while not necessarily written for or about J, nonetheless reminds me of how she seemed to feel about that silly yet quite endearing cat.

Cheesiest

I dislike cheesy,
but for you I will fly past the
boundaries of the cheesiest, sappiest, craziest, sloppiest
poems, songs, and movies
till you see how very cheesy I can be.
But only for you.

I dislike Dr. Pepper,
but for you I will drink
more of that fizzy, syrupy, too sweet
beverage than
the biggest Dr. Pepper fan in the world.
But only for you.

I dislike winter,
but for you I will make
snow angels and snowmen, string lights, and
fishtail down the road on my way to work
every day
for the rest of my life.
But only for you.

I dislike hay,
but for you I will
sneeze, cough, gag,
have asthma, and try to avoid
rubbing my eyes.

But only for you.

So if you're in the market for a cheesy,
Dr. Pepper–drinking,
snowman building,
sneezing, coughing girl,
then I'm the girl for you.

But if you still like me without all that …
well, that's okay too.

A Tendency toward Reclusiveness

With her creativity came a natural reclusiveness. She spent hours in her room or her apartment reading, drawing, painting, and developing ideas.

Of Dreams

We wake

suddenly,

with a night's worth

of dreams

boiling out of

gaping

and

astonished

mouths

in silent screams

against the constricting

envelope

of

darkness.

Fog

Fog descends

once

again,

like smoke without the flame.

So dense

I cannot see

the sky.

She did, however, love to go out with her friends and cousins for coffee, a meal, and to sing karaoke. While she never liked to drink, she did love to sing. She occasionally went to local karaoke bars for the opportunity to observe life and participate in it through singing. She sat back and drew what she observed while waiting for her next opportunity to sing.

If Wishes Were

Last night I wished upon a star
that I'd awake
in your arms.
The birds would cheep outside

our door,

and we'd be together

forevermore.

This morning I woke

to an empty bed

and cried awhile

with my teddy bear;

then got me up and went to work.

(Tonight I'll wish for world peace instead.)

Her best friend, Selena (or Alice, as Janet called her), frequently encouraged her to come out of her reclusiveness to experience life as it was happening. To try on new clothes, do new things, or go new places. Janet frequently spoke of how Selena encouraged her to walk on the Greenbelt, where they would laugh, skip, swing, and just have fun. Once Janet called Selena and asked her to pick her up to go to the hospital. Selena asked her why, and Janet explained how she had thrown her hip out while doing the twist in her apartment. They laughed so hard over that as Selena drove her to the hospital.

Night Magic

Night magic…

as darkness falls,
a curtain drawn,
shutting out intruders to the
secret lantern burning in my depths.
I sit alone by an
open window to the world that is night
and listen to
softly spoken
whispers,
too silent to be considered
sound.
The soft and gentle breeze
sighs through the trees.
Moonlight touches down upon the grass.
All these things call to me
as the autumn leaves do their gypsy dance.

"Come out and play with us;
run and skip and sing and twirl and dance
with us till you are shrouded in the indefinable
mist
of a late autumn night
the scent of freedom."

And as if in a trance,
I find myself outdoors,
running and skipping and singing and twirling and dancing
with roots wild at my feet,
and branches clutching at my hem,
as though they were open arms
welcoming me home.

Life, Death, and Learning

Life is frequently full of loss and grief. Janet had more than her share of loss. After a friend died, she wrote the following poem.

On the Death of a Friend

How mysterious

that one who was so recently full of bloom

and beauty

could in a mere instant not be so.

A memory of then restless hands.

You nonchalantly shrugged off inconvenience

Every day.

Oh, my dear.

My friend.

You are beyond inconvenience now.

Your journey has only begun,

And I will meet you on some tree-lined path

On a distant afternoon.

Grief

Growing Up

When I was a child, I thought like a child.

Spring grass meant anticipation then.

The blossoming tulips heralded a sense of freedom.

Free from work and study.

Freedom of imagination. (We built imagination on top of itself and into

another world.)

We mimicked our elders, never envisioning a day when it would

no longer be mimicry.

Oh, those irresponsible days

full of wonder and vivacity.

Momentary joy in every moment.

We knew no fear—as was apparent from our antics.

What monkeys we were as children,

ceaselessly playing and mock brawling.

How could we have known that it would ever not be so?

Even later into my teens and twenties,

in the infancy of my adulthood,

maturity itself held no real meaning.

A lark.

A role to playact till it grew bothersome,

and then back to the bosom of home and hearth.

Childhood had not departed, not quite.

There was a time when I knew absolutely everything!

How intelligent was I!

For my experiences were the first experienccs (or so I assumed), and

no one could ever feel the same.

So much intensity!

I dreaded being understood so much more than being misunderstood.

For misunderstanding made me original.

But I did not understand that at the time.

Now I realize that I am not uncommon.

Since the beginning of time, of the human race,

every soul has thought herself to be the first, and I was no exception.

I invented love, self-loathing, fear, regard, respect, insecurity, anticipation … and none were felt

before; how else could they be so fresh to me?

I know now that I am average.

All those emotions were fresh simply because I was fresh.

And my much-lauded intelligence?

A joke for all I really know

is that I know "absolutely" nothing compared with what there is to know.

And that I will never experience enough heartbeats or brain waves to learn even a fraction of

life.

Hopes and Dreams

Journaling was always an important part of emotional release and self-expression that Janet utilized throughout her teen years and adulthood. She was able to express a wide range of emotions, in addition to detailing daily happenings and life dreams. At the age of nineteen she recognized that she experienced her greatest happiness when she was writing, painting, and playing her violin.

"Now here's my dream. Promise not to laugh? I want to write a book. Poetry and such first. But later, later I want, so badly, to write a <u>Real</u> book. Not a novel, but a, well, I guess a novel. But not a mystery or romance, or anything like that. An introspective type of book. Maybe stream of consciousness, or journal–like, and I want to succeed. But I don't know if I can do it. You see, I want to share with others how I felt on a dark night in August when the colorful leaves were transformed to gray-black with the loss of the Sun's energy. How the stars hung faintly, and the entire valley was plunged into a strange and everchanging, yet somehow still, unbelievably still, dreamworld. I want them after reading it, to feel (or while reading it) as if they were there, sitting with me outside watching the blue smoke trail up and fade into the shadows from the bright end of my cigarette. To wonder at the transformation. To sip cocoa in front of a campfire while searching with my eyes behind every tree for some new and wonderful sign of life. A rustling, we jump together, imagining bears and hoping for a deer to wander into view. I want to feel connected, as if I have made some mark on the world which allows my heart to flow its life blood through the imagination and heart of my readers.

Do you know what I mean?" Love Janet Cole.

Janet adamantly denied any serious plan to ever marry, stating the only way she would ever get married, "is if I were to meet just the right person for me in every way." However, she spent significant time in detailing in pictures and words the wedding dress and accessories she hoped to wear someday. She wrote, "Blue and Pink (representing man & woman, obviously) will be the wedding colors. But I don't want to be stuck with 2 concrete shades of the colors." She also wrote and drew in detail the wedding cake and reception she dreamed to have in a park.

Yet Another Romantic Melodrama

Enclosures round mine heart endured through winter, spring, and fall;
but with the summer's torrid 'brace came openness and leafy grace
of pathways strewn round rosy shrub.

And lined along the stony road grew gatherings of silver'd sedge,
till once converged below the hill the road bespies a loch.

Oft times, as summer's heat did wilt the proudest blooms
in afternoons of wanton fire and cloudless sky,
two lovers did find solitude and sanctu'ry 'neath bower made
of willow leaves by gentle shore.

Me thinks we lov'd the summer 'way, though I remember not its burn
(as I was safe in cool, sweet bliss, my love's bright eyes my only sun).

One morn a galey wind arose to tear apart that hallowed place
where love first grew, and kisses fell like rain about our entwin'd forms.

My love did not appear that day; nor upon the next.
And when a sennight's minutes tick'd away in solitude,
I realized the leaves had changed, grown full, and gilded on their branch.

Summer's shades had rusted, and as autumn's grasp took o'er the land,
my heart's gate shut, and ivy grew round the locks and hid away
the place where once a love I knew.

Love, Familial and Romantic

There is frequently a struggle in accepting ourselves that is bound up in how we love and how we are loved. Janet had occasions in her life where she trusted and loved someone in spite of deep personal pain. Albeit usually unintentional, this pain was brought on by the overwhelming expectations and judgments she experienced from her loved ones. Sometimes the ones closest to us hurt us the most.

Rejection

A leaf shakes in sorrow as
the twig
that it clung to
(so tightly)
shoves it away.

Sister Sue the Sunshine Girl

A child of divorce, Janet was vulnerable to that pain because she wanted so much to have a relationship that did not wind up in divorce. She had her heart broken more than once and was determined to not rush into anything without being sure.

Evacuee

It is impossible to maintain my love for you
against such conditions/
To survive, love needs both sun and shade/
But you, with your intensity and bright passion,
have burned me to the very root/

You demand constant attention/
You expect perfection/
You want me as you want me, not as I am/

Your love for me has become a painful burden, a catastrophic event/

So I am left with no other choice but to evacuate my heart
for its own protection.

Faith

Faith was a difficult concept for Janet. She accepted Christ as a young adult and was baptized. However, she frequently vacillated, questioned God, and prayed to him throughout the years. Like Thomas, at times she wanted to see the nail marks in Christ's palm and wrist.

You Speak

You speak of love as if it were
tangible.
But I have difficulty seeing reality in a thing unseen.

Even were it's existence proven
conclusively,
how can one hold
something as elusive as love—as flighty as forever
in a hand that even now as we speak has decayed
(infinitesimally)?

But you speak of love as if it were
a tangible thing.

Suddenly, I find myself—the cynic—wanting to believe
so badly.

What kind of illusionist are you?
For you speak of love,
and I want to believe despite all proof to the contrary.

Holding my hand out,
foolishly reaching for something
I could never hope to touch.

As Janet's mom, I always wanted to offer her support and hope. I wanted so much for her to understand her beauty and to understand faith. While I tried to understand her perspective, it was always difficult and ultimately heartbreaking for me to hear her talk of being agnostic and even atheist. I knew that the decision of faith is a very personal decision and one that a mother cannot make for her child. I knew all I could do was to continue to pray for guidance and to offer her my unconditional love as her mother.

Albatross

I don't know why, but whenever I pray,

I feel as though I am calling down from the top of a well,

and then, just waiting for my own voice—

thin,
diminished—

to drift, echoing back to me

with fewer answers in it than when first uttered.

How much life can one soul contain?

How much anguish, fear,

and guilt before

bursting, it begins the inevitable collapse

helped out of existence by its own volume?

I feel as though my life were crowding in and suffocating me,

like bricks heaped one by one upon the chest of the accused heretic

until there remains but one choice—

make false confession… or die!

I refuse to feel guilt for that which I never requested.

I contain the world in my soul,

but it does not contain me.

There is no place in this world for a misplaced poet.

No hollow carved especially in my shape that I can fit perfectly into.

So I wander through the world out of sorts and grizzly.

Look, it's the ash girl!

Can you spot her gray, cracking face?

Look quickly for any second she might crumble into dust.

(It's not often you see someone cremated by her own bitterness.)

Maybe you want to take a photograph.

My mouth opens, and black soot issues forth.

My tongue is stained from it, and my throat dry from lack of water.

Still, I find the saliva and bite my very arm for thirst

to make my defense heard.

Acceptance

Janet, as we all do, wanted to be accepted for who she was.

I Want

I want to be graceful,
respected,
beautiful,
loved,
drunk.
Perfect.

I want to be there when things happen.
I want to disappear,
lose weight.
I want closure,
forgiveness.
I want to be perfect.

Perfect, soft- but well spoken,
eloquent,
neat and tidy,
kind, compassionate,
empathetic,
intelligent,
and with an excellent sense of timing and
direction.

I want to be perfect—
good handwriting,
happy,
nymph like,
quiet, graceful, still,
like Ophelia in a lake.
Like a Lord Byron poem:
to "walk in beauty."
Like a movie wherein the heroine never farts or belches,
in which the bathroom
has no need of a toilet.
Waiflike, elvish,

perfect.
Beautiful even in a gunnysack.

Reflection and Healing

Life is a series of events, along which come natural opportunities for reflecting on our past in the hope of renewing ourselves into stronger healthier individuals for our future. Janet, in her natural solitude, was always willing to look back to gain something new and fresh.

Revisited

So strange—
the Spokane that lived so fondly in my memory
does not quite match the reality.
Smaller now … noisier streets … and the people like ants,
fighting over bits of gravel, parking spaces, and a lungful of smoggy air.
From my hotel room, I have an excellent view of the writhing masses
in their city of numerous tunnels.

Carrying three times their own weight in
responsibility,
anger,
guilt,
and shopping bags full of small to medium household appliances.

So small against the sky outside the glass.

The sun sets, and darkness oozes over tall and short buildings alike.
Shiny new steel and glass frames squat next to dingy and worn brick
(without quite making eye contact).

Peace.
Abnormal after years of internal conflict.
It's odd.
Sometimes the cessation of cannon fire
rings louder than the actual blast.

Janet was so willing to accept and love someone in spite of pain and hurt. She frequently encouraged her family to love and not hold judgment against someone for having been hurt.

Argument for Love

Love is a bittersweet thing.
Often painful,
always alarming.
For how could it not be unnerving to
open oneself up to the highest form of vulnerability?
To trust another with your very soul?
Love is difficult—definitely.

But if you can force yourself beyond the fear, it can also be the most liberating
emotion in existence.
Ripe with possibility, vividness, and beauty.

Love defies definition because with every occurrence, each manifestation,
it changes.

Regardless of anything else, love is worth the risk of pain, the fear of rejection

(simply for its own sake).

Cancer

Janet moved to California to live with us after she was provisionally diagnosed with Hodgkin's lymphoma. Giving up her home and lifestyle was very difficult for her and meant quite an adjustment. However; she quickly made new friends. Our friends quickly became her friends, second moms, friends who prayed for her, and stayed by her through thick and thin. In addition, she maintained steady contact with her dear family and friends from the Boise area, around the country, and even the world who also continued to pray, support, and encourage her.

We were all so amazed at her strength in times of great difficulty and physical pain. Her greatest desire was to recover from the wickedness of the disease and return to her beloved hometown of Boise.

Though I Never Chose This Path
I refuse to turn from it in fear.

There is nothing in my past for me to reach for.
Somehow I must cleave a new way through the crawling snakes and
writhing eels.
I must make a wind of my own determination to safely
guide me into the future.

One thing, though.
I will never again wear my anguish, guilt, and pain around my neck
for all to see and mock.

Janet at Tiverton House in Los Angeles, California, getting treatment.

Unfortunately, the side effects of all the treatment were too much for her heart.

Psalm 62:5–6 states, "Find Rest, O my Soul, in God alone; my hope comes from him. He alone is my rock and my salvation; he is my fortress, I will not be shaken."

There is hope, however, in a compassionate Almighty God who understands our questions and struggles. My prayer is in the ultimate hope in Christ Jesus, that one day I will be reunited with him, and will see my darling daughter, Janet Sue Cole, again. At that time, it will be in our Lord God's heavenly meadows made for all His children, with a heavenly array of glorious colors and images more than all the meadows that Janet had ever hoped to imagine.

Janet Sue Cole, Summer 2011

You are my sunshine,
My only sunshine.
You make me happy,
When the skies are gray.
You'll never know dear,
How much I love you.

Jimmie Davis and Charles Mitchell

2000, Yellowstone National Park

Conclusion

I thank the Good Lord for giving Janet to me. She was a blessing in my life and will always be my sunshine girl.

ACKNOWLEDGMENTS

I would like to express deep appreciation for all those who provided support for Janet during her time in treatment. The support that Janet and I as her mother received from her treatment team at Kern Medical Center Oncology Unit in Bakersfield, CA under direction of Dr. David Kanamori, MD and Shane Tu, MD, along with her primary pharmaceutical physician Ali Bazmi, Pharm.D., BCOP was overwhelmingly professional, thorough and kind. There were also the many nurses and staff that ultimately shared their professional nursing skills, empathy and ultimate friendship to my dear Janet including: Kara Shaw, RN who would go with Janet to sing Karaoke after hours, Nancy, Eileen, Betty, and so many others involved in her care. Janet always said she would rather get her treatment at KMC oncology than anywhere else in the area. In addition, Kern Medical Center residency inpatient team under the direction of Dr. Navin M. Amin, MD Chief of Residency were committed to treating Janet with kindness and dedication to care under frequently overwhelming circumstances.

I would like to thank the treatment team at the Ronald Reagan University of California Los Angeles under direction of UCLA Physician Sven de Vos, M.D., Ph.D. who assisted Janet, me, and our family through the process of her stem cell transplant. The dedication to care was exemplified throughout the treatment process. There was nothing better than knowing as a family member and patient that one did not have to undergo extreme expenses or stress by traveling back and forth between home and hospital, or incurring expensive costs of hotel bills while receiving treatment outside of the home area. The Tiverton House was such a space in being able to be within walking distance of the hospital. It afforded not only the proximity but also a home away from home. It was a place where we had opportunity to meet others in similar situations. It was a place where we could stay with Janet while she remained close to her treatment program.

I would also like to thank my dear friends and former Riverlakes Church & Bible study home group members who prayed with myself, Janet and our family during Janet's treatment and beyond her passing. Gary and Patsy Grijalva, Greg and Elaine Hull, Ken and Shelly Wonderly and their daughter Rachael Ward, Dale and Pat Simkins, Andrew and Maria Farkus, Brian and Debbie Prendez, Mike and Dina Kretsinger, Chad and Tracy Dixon, and many others provided support during those very difficult years and several of whom provided specific encouragement for my writing this book. My dear friend Patsy was an ever constant in support and love who shared her personal involvement in the Leukemia and Lymphoma Society Light the Night. This opened my eyes to ways people can get involved in research treatment while honoring the memory of our loved ones.

I thank Elaine Hull for taking so much of her time to provide support and friendship to Janet during her treatment, and for writing the foreword for this book. Janet frequently talked of her appreciation for Elaine and on August 26, 2011, just barely over one month before she passed away, she wrote in her journal about getting around "for an exciting day with my friend Elaine Hull. After she picked me up at 1030 am we ran a few errands that had been pressing on me, and then enjoyed a lovely luncheon at the French Café "Mimis" which we both love so much. We sat for quite some time over lunch talking and then headed to the mall."

As the mother of a daughter lost to a diagnosis of Hodgkin's Lymphoma and a daughter of a mother lost to pancreatic cancer, I was more than fortunate to find an avenue of emotional release and expression of my loss and grief through getting involved in the Bakersfield Leukemia and Lymphoma Society Team in Training group under Jane Lutz, coordinator. There was nothing like the sweat equity of training for and running/walking a marathon in the San Francisco 2012 Nike Women's Marathon: A race to benefit the Leukemia Lymphoma Society to release the built-up emotional energy of 3 years of dealing with the devastating impact of cancer treatment. Coach Michele

McDermott taught me that there is nothing wrong with stopping to capture a picture during training, to allow time to soak in the whole experience. Mike Gloss and Linda Thomure-Monje were my coaches during the training for and completing the 2013 Bass Lake Triathlon, which wound up being the most fulfilling team experience I have been through. Through Team in Training I had the opportunity to meet many new friends with similar hearts and similar compulsions; also, to see the overwhelming commitment of family and friends who came to cheer me on to the end. Ultimately to help find a cure.

I would like to thank my dear aunt, Janet Miller and my Finnish niece, Anna Junnila who read through an initial version of this book and Janet's poetry, sharing a lasting memory and providing critical feedback during the process of this book. I thank FedEx team member Kiana Powell at the Lone Tree Brentwood, California store and to Mike's Camera - Pleasant Hill team member Chey Hewitt, for their assistance and careful scanning of Janet's art work. Their appreciation for the meaning of these pieces was appreciated. It has been a pleasure to work with the talented people at Westbow publishing. I appreciate their expertise and helping me in the process of completing this project.

I would also like to thank those who kept Janet's hopes alive in her desire to return to full health and ultimately to her home in Boise, Idaho. To her father, Dennis Cole, who kept in regular daily contact with her throughout. Janet loved her best friend, Selena (Ashby) Jungling. She so loved the time they spent together in Boise and during Selena's visit to California. As her mother, I will always be grateful for the special friendship they shared. I also appreciate the close bond Janet experienced with her cousins: Alethia Dahlin, Heather Reese and Amanda Cole. Janet was so happy when her step-sister in-law Brie Marshall, came to California and made a point to visit her. I would like to thank my parents Jonas and Mary Lee, who always loved and supported Janet and came and stayed with her during the summer of 2011. Janet loved each of you and enjoyed calling and talking to you nearly daily. To each of the other cousins, aunts and uncles, on both her fathers and mother's side, Janet loved you, as do I.

I thank my son and Janet's brother, James Cole (and his wife Katy) who always loved and was loved by his sister and myself. Jim provided me physical help with design of this book, along with constructive criticism reminding me to stay true to Janet throughout. I know that Janet would so love to have met her nephew Quincy and niece Jovie Sue.

To Janet's step-sister, Kailey Hicks, who shared her teen years, her youth for better and worse in our home, living and learning of the impact cancer has on a family's daily routines.

Finally, I thank my wonderful husband, David Harder who gives me his love and full support with a dash of constructive feedback in the writing of this book. I appreciate his sharing time with me back and forth between work and being with Janet throughout her course of treatment. His love of Janet grew through the time he had to spend with her as her stepfather. He frequently speaks of the time he spent with Janet at Tiverton House while getting treatment in the summer of 2011. They shared talks from absolutely nothing, little things, to more serious discussion of their individual beliefs. They and we spent hours together, cruising through town on the UCLA shuttle, or pushing her in her wheelchair through the streets of Westwood to and from her treatments and even to and from the hospital gift shop where she shopped for wigs, scarves and just doing some window shopping.

Thank you all,

Deb

The author participating in a Team in Training Triathlon event to benefit the Leukemia and Lymphoma Society in 2013. She encourages individuals to get involved in supporting cancer treatment and research.

Printed in the United States
By Bookmasters